978-0931-798047
AF570729

SOYBEAN COOKERY

BY

VIRG AND JO LEMLEY

SECOND EDITION

WILDERNESS HOUSE

2656 CIRCLE DRIVE

ESCONDIDO CA

© COPYRIGHT

1975

ALL RIGHTS RESERVED

FOR OUR CHILDREN ——————

DEBORAH
SUZANNE
KIRK

AT WILDERNESS HOUSE

WE TRIED COOKING WITH THE SOYBEAN LONG AGO. WE BOUGHT EVERY COOKBOOK WE COULD FIND ON THE SOYBEAN AND FOUND THAT IT JUST WASN T OUR FAVORITE FOOD. BUT THE HIGH NUTRITIONAL VALUE AND LOW COST ASPECT OF THIS BEAN KEPT HAUNTING US. SO— WE SET OUT TO FIND A WAY TO MAKE IT MORE PALATABLE. THIS IS WHAT SOYBEAN COOKERY IS ALL ABOUT.

WILDERNESS HOUSE SOYBEAN TIPS

- SOYBEANS COMBINE MORE CONCENTRATED FOOD ELEMENTS THAN ANY OTHER COMMON FOOD. THEY ARE RICH IN MINERALS, B VITAMINS, CONTAIN ALL OF THE AMINO ACIDS, AND LECITHIN THAT HELPS THE BODY BREAK DOWN CHOLESTEROL. SOYBEANS CONTAIN AN AVERAGE OF 40 % CRUDE PROTEIN—MORE THAN TWICE AS MUCH AS BEEF OR FISH, THREE TIMES MORE THAN EGGS OR WHOLE WHEAT FLOUR, AND ELEVEN TIMES MORE THAN WHOLE MILK.

- SOYBEANS RELUCTANTLY ABSORB OTHER FLAVORS. THEY ARE VERY INDEPENDENT AND HOLD ON TO THEIR NUTTY FLAVOR. WE FOUND THAT CINNAMON NEUTRALIZES THIS. OTHER SPICES THAT DO WELL WITH THE SOYBEAN ARE OREGANO, BASIL, ROSEMARY, CHILI POWDER, CUMIN, AND DILL.

- MOST SOYBEAN RECIPES ARE BETTER MADE AHEAD SO THAT SUBTLE FLAVORS WILL PENETRATE THAT STUBBORN BEAN. WE HAVE STIPULATED RECIPES THAT WE FEEL MUST BE MADE IN ADVANCE FOR A PERFECT BLENDING OF FLAVORS.

- WE ALWAYS KEEP SOME COOKED SOYBEANS IN OUR FREEZER IN TWO CUP PACKETS SO THAT WE ARE WELL PREPARED TO MAKE A SOYBEAN DISH IN A HURRY. AND SOYBEAN CASSEROLES ARE A NATURAL FOR PREPARING AHEAD AND FREEZING.

- IT TAKES ONE-FOURTH THE AMOUNT OF ENERGY TO COOK SOYBEANS WITH A PRESSURE COOKER THAN BY CONVENTIONAL METHODS. USE BASIC SOYBEAN METHOD NO. 1 IF YOU HAVE A PRESSURE COOKER AND BASIC SOYBEAN METHOD NO. 2 IF YOU DON'T.

- AT WILDERNESS HOUSE WE USUALLY USE A BLENDER TO PUREE OUR SOYBEANS. WE PUT THE SOYBEANS IN THE BLENDER WITH ONE OF THE LIQUIDS FROM THE RECIPE (OIL, EGGS, MILK, ETC.) AND PUREE THEM. THEY MAY ALSO BE PUREED WITH A SIEVE.

- IF YOU FIND THAT SOYBEANS, LIKE OTHER BEANS CAUSE YOU GASTRIC DISTURBANCE SIMPLY ADD 1/2 TEASPOON BAKING SODA TO THE BASIC SOYBEAN RECIPE. THIS DOES DESTROY A MINIMAL AMOUNT OF THE ENZYMES — SO IT IS OPTIONAL.

- NO—AT WILDERNESS HOUSE WE ARE NOT VEGETARIANS BUT WE RARELY USE EXPENSIVE MEAT ANYMORE, EXCEPT FOR FLAVORING, SINCE WE DISCOVERED THE SECRETS OF SOYBEAN COOKERY.

TABLE OF CONTENTS

BASIC SOYBEAN RECIPE

2 C. DRIED SOYBEANS
6 C. WATER
1 1/2 TSP. SALT
1/2 TSP. BAKING SODA (OPTIONAL)

METHOD NO. 1

PUT INGREDIENTS IN A 6 QUART PRESSURE COOKER AND COOK UNDER PRESSURE FOR ONE HOUR.

METHOD NO. 2

COMBINE INGREDIENTS AND LET STAND IN THE REFRIGERATOR OVERNIGHT. THEN SIMMER FOR FOUR HOURS. ADD ADDITIONAL WATER, AS REQUIRED.

IF A RECIPE SAYS TO TOSS ALL INGREDIENTS IN THE PRESSURE COOKER, YOU MAY USE METHOD NO. 2 BY SOAKING YOUR SOYBEANS OVERNIGHT— THEN ADDING THE OTHER INGREDIENTS AND SIMMER FOR FOUR HOURS.

CROCK POT METHOD

COMBINE THE ABOVE INGREDIENTS AND PUT IN YOUR CROCK POT ON LOW, OVERNIGHT (12 HOURS). THE FOLLOWING MORNING ASSEMBLE YOUR RECIPE, MODIFIED BY YOUR CROCK POT INSTRUCTIONS. COOK ON HIGH FOR 1 HOUR AND LOW FOR 10 TO 12 HOURS, THEN SERVE.

YIELDS 5 CUPS OF COOKED SOYBEANS.

ROASTED SOYBEANS HEALTHY-MUNCHY

2 C. DRIED SOYBEANS
8 C. WATER
1 TSP. SALT
2 TBS. OLIVE OIL

SOAK SOYBEANS IN SALTED WATER OVERNIGHT. DRAIN WELL AND BLOT DRY WITH A TOWEL. SPREAD SOYBEANS IN A 9 X 12 PAN OR A LARGE ROUND SKILLET. PUT IN A 200° OVEN FOR 2 HOURS, STIRRING OCCASIONALLY. THEN ADD OLIVE OIL AND SALT SOYBEANS TO TASTE. RETURN SOYBEANS TO OVEN UNDER HOT BROILER. STIR EVERY 30 SECONDS UNDER BROILER UNTIL THE SOYBEANS ARE A DEEP GOLDEN BROWN— ABOUT 5 MINUTES. STORE IN AIR-TIGHT CONTAINER.

IF YOUR ROASTED SOYBEANS AREN'T DRY ENOUGH, OR IF THEY COLLECT MOISTURE FROM THE AIR, PLACE THEM IN THE OVEN AT 350° FOR 15 MINUTES.

GOOD SERVED HOT FOR A SNACK OR SERVED AS YOU WOULD PEANUTS. CAN BE GROUND AND ADDED TO COOKIES AND OTHER DISHES TO ADD CRUNCHINESS AND PROTEIN. EXCELLENT IN A PARTY MIX.

MAKES 2 CUPS
PROTEIN: 165 GRAMS

ZIPPY DIP

2 C. COOKED SOYBEANS—DRAINED
2 TBS. OLIVE OIL
3 TBS. LEMON JUICE
1/4 TSP. SALT
1/2 TSP. MINCED GARLIC
3 TBS. MINCED ONIONS

PUREE BEANS, COMBINE WITH OTHER INGREDIENTS. CHILL FOR SEVERAL HOURS AND SERVE.

MAKES 2 CUPS
PROTEIN: 67 GRAMS

MEXICAN DIP

1 C. COOKED SOYBEANS — DRAINED
1 C. SOUR CREAM
2 TBS. MINCED ONIONS
1 CAN, 4 OZ., DICED GREEN CHILES
1/4 TSP. CHILI POWDER
1/8 TSP. CUMIN
1/4 TSP. SALT
DASH OF TABASCO SAUCE
DASH OF CAYENNE PEPPER

MASH SOYBEANS—BLEND IN REMAINING INGREDIENTS. CHILL FOR SEVERAL HOURS BEFORE SERVING. SERVE WITH TACO CHIPS PAGE 7.

MAKES 2 CUPS
PROTEIN: 39 GRAMS

CHEESE BALLS

2 C. COOKED SOYBEANS — DRAINED
1 EGG BEATEN
2 TBS. MINCED ONION
1 CAN (4 OZ.) GREEN CHILES — DRAINED
1/2 C. PARMESAN CHEESE
1 TBS. WHOLE WHEAT FLOUR
1/4 TSP. SALT
1 TSP. CHILI POWDER
1/4 POUND CHEDDAR CHEESE — CUBED
1/4 C. SESAME SEED
OR
1/4 C. CORN MEAL
OIL — FOR DEEP FRYING

MASH SOYBEANS AND COMBINE WITH EGG, ONION, CHILES, PARMESAN CHEESE, FLOUR, SALT, AND CHILI POWDER. MAKE A BALL OF THIS MIXTURE — AROUND EACH CUBE OF CHEDDAR CHEESE. ROLL BALL IN SESAME SEEDS OR CORN MEAL. DEEP FRY AT MEDIUM HEAT, FOR ABOUT 3 MINUTES, SO THAT THE CHEESE BALL WILL BE A DARK GOLDEN BROWN AND THE CHEESE INSIDE MELTS. DRAIN AND LET SIT FOR 3 OR 4 MINUTES BEFORE SERVING.........OR.....CHILL FOR SEVERAL HOURS AND SERVE COLD.

CHEESEBALLS 12-16
PROTEIN: 129 GRAMS

SANDWICH SPREAD

BEATS BOLOGNA

1 C. SOYBEAN — MASHED
2 TBS. MAYONNAISE
2 TBS. PICKLE RELISH
2 TBS. MINCED GREEN ONION
PINCH OF SALT

MIX TOGETHER WELL AND CHILL FOR 3 OR MORE HOURS. SPREAD ON BREAD FOR SANDWICH.

SERVES: 4
PROTEIN: 34 GRAMS

PERFECTION SALAD

1 ENVELOPE UNFLAVORED GELATIN
1 1/4 C. COLD WATER
2 CUBES CHICKEN BOUILLON
2 TBS. VINEGAR
3 TBS. LEMON JUICE
1/4 C. SUGAR
1 C. COOKED SOYBEANS— DRAINED
1 C. RAW CABBAGE — SHREDDED
1 C. RAW CARROT— SHREDDED
1 TBS. BELL PEPPER MINCED

SPRINKLE GELATIN OVER COLD WATER. PLACE OVER LOW HEAT. STIR CONSTANTLY UNTIL GELATIN DISOLVES, ABOUT 3 MINUTES. STIR IN BOUILLON, VINEGAR, LEMON JUICE, AND SUGAR. STIR UNTIL DISSOLVED. PUT IN MOLD IN REFRIGERATOR UNTIL IT STARTS TO SET. STIR IN VEGETABLES AND CHILL 4 HOURS HOURS OR MORE.

SERVES: 6
PROTEIN: 42 GRAMS

TACO SALAD

DELIGHT YOUR GUESTS

TOSS AND CHILL:

2 C. COOKED SOYBEANS — DRAINED
3 C. SHREDDED LETTUCE
2 TOMATOES — FINELY DICED
1/2 C. SLICED OLIVES
1/4 C. MINCED GREEN ONION
1 C. GRATED CHEDDAR CHEESE
1/4 TSP. SALT
1/2 C. DICED GREEN CHILES

BLEND AND CHILL FOR DRESSING:

1 LARGE AVOCADO MASHED — ABOUT 1 CUP
1/2 TSP. CHILI POWDER
1/4 TSP. CUMIN
1/4 TSP. SALT
1/2 C. SOUR CREAM
DASH OF TABASCO SAUCE
1/2 TSP. LEMON JUICE

JUST BEFORE SERVING PUT ON THE DRESSING AND TOSS ALL INGREDIENTS WITH 1/2 CUP CRUSHED CORN CHIPS.

SERVES: 6
PROTEIN: 102 GRAMS

THIS IS PERFECT FOR A MAIN DISH AND ABSOLUTELY DELICIOUS SERVED IN A STEAMED TORTILLA.

CORN CHIPS (FOR THE TACO SALAD)

CUT 4 CORN TORTILLAS INTO 1 INCH SQUARES. FRY CHIPS IN HOT OIL UNTIL GOLDEN, TURNING SEVERAL TIMES. SPRINKLE WITH SALT AND CHILI POWDER JUST BEFORE REMOVING FROM THE PAN. DRAIN WELL. CRUSH WITH A ROLLING PIN FOR THE SALAD.

PICNIC SALAD

2 C. COOKED SOYBEANS — DRAINED
1/2 C. SLICED OLIVES
1/2 C. FINELY CHOPPED CELERY
1/4 C. FINELY CHOPPED ONIONS
1 TSP. VINEGAR
4 BOILED EGGS — CHOPPED
1/4 C. MAYONNIASE
1/4 C. SWEET PICKLE RELISH
1/2 TSP. COARSE BLACK PEPPER

MIX ALL INGREDIENTS IN A BOWL. CHILL FOR 4 OR MORE HOURS.

SERVES: 4-6
PROTEIN: 91 GRAMS

TRY OUR PICNIC SALAD INSTEAD OF POTATO SALAD.

SOYBEAN BOWL

2 C. COOKED SOYBEANS — DRAINED
1 1/2 C. CELERY — FINELY CHOPPED
1/2 C. SWEET PICKLE RELISH
1/2 C. SALAD OIL
2 TBS. ONION — FINELY CHOPPED
2 TSP. DIJON MUSTARD
2 TBS. GREEN PEPPER — MINCED

MARINATE OVERNIGHT. SERVE IN BOWLS. SALT TO TASTE.

SERVES: 4-6
PROTEIN: 68 GRAMS

BEACH SALAD

2 C. COOKED SOYBEANS — DRAINED
1 CAN CHUNK TUNA
1/2 C. CELERY — THINLY SLICED
1/2 C. DILL PICKLE — COARSELY CHOPPED
1/2 TSP. SALT
1/8 TSP. BLACK PEPPER
1 TSP. PARSLEY
1/4 C. MAYONNAISE

TOSS INGREDIENTS TOGETHER. CHILL 4 OR MORE HOURS. SERVE ON FRILLY LETTUCE AND GARNISH WITH EGG SLICES.

SERVES: 4-6
PROTEIN: 115 GRAMS

SPROUT SALAD

1 1/4 C. COOKED SOYBEANS — DRAINED
1/2 C. GRATED ZUCCHINI
1/2 C. SOYBEAN SPROUTS
1/4 C. CIDER VINEGAR
1 TBS. HONEY
1/2 TSP. SALT
2 TBS. ONION — FINELY DICED
2 TSP. MINCED GINGER ROOT

COMBINE AND CHILL AT LEAST 4 HOURS BEFORE SERVING.

SERVES: 4
PROTEIN: 47 GRAMS

WILDERNESS HOUSE SLAW

2 1/2 C. COOKED SOYBEANS — DRAINED
1 C. SHREDDED CABBAGE
3/4 C. CARROT — COARSELY GRATED
2/3 C. MAYONNAISE
1/2 TSP. SALT
1/2 TSP. DIJON MUSTARD
1 TBS. HORSERADISH
1/2 TSP. ALLSPICE
1 TSP. WORCESTERSHIRE SAUCE
1/2 TSP. COARSE PEPPER
2 TSP. LEMON JUICE

COMBINE SOYBEANS CABBAGE AND CARROT. COMBINE REMAINING INGREDIENTS IN A SEPARATE BOWL, THEN MIX WITH VEGETABLES. CHILL FOR AT LEAST 4 HOURS.

SERVES: 4-6
PROTEIN: 84 GRAMS

SHEPHERD'S SOUP

2 C. DRIED SOYBEANS
6 C. WATER
1/4 C. OLIVE OIL
2 TSP. ALLSPICE
2 TSP. SALT
1/2 TSP. CURRY POWDER
1 C. CHOPPED BELL PEPPER
1 C. CHOPPED ONION
1 C. DICED CELERY
2 C. SLICED ZUCCHINI
1 CAN (28 OZ.) WHOLE TOMATOES

PUT ALL INGREDIENTS IN PRESSURE COOKER AND COOK UNDER PRESSURE FOR 1 HOUR. IF YOU DO NOT HAVE A PRESSURE COOKER USE METHOD NO. 2 (PAGE 1).

SERVES: 6
PROTEIN: 176 GRAMS

CHEESE SOUP MOM'S FAVORITE

3 C. COOKED SOYBEANS MASHED
1 LARGE CAN (46 OZ.) TOMATO JUICE
1 TBS. WORCESTERSHIRE SAUCE
1 TBS. SOY SAUCE
1/2 TSP. TABASCO SAUCE
2 C. MONTEREY JACK CHEESE — GRATED

COMBINE SOYBEANS, TOMATO JUICE, AND SPICES. SIMMER FOR 30 MINUTES, STIRRING OCCASIONALLY. JUST BEFORE SERVING, STIR IN CHEESE.

SERVES: 4-6
PROTEIN: 135 GRAMS

WILDERNESS HOUSE SOUP

2 C. COOKED SOYBEANS
2 1/2 C. CHICKEN BROTH
1/2 C. FINELY CHOPPED CELERY LEAVES
1/2 C. FINELY CHOPPED ONION
1/8 TSP. COARSE PEPPER
PINCH OF SALT

SIMMER INGREDIENTS FOR 30 MINUTES. SERVE HOT. MAY BE MADE AHEAD.

SERVES: 6
PROTEIN: 66 GRAMS

SOUTHERN BISQUE

2 C. COOKED SOYBEANS
1 1/2 C. HALF AND HALF CREAM
1 C. BOILING WATER
2 CHICKEN BOUILLON CUBES
2 TBS. MINCED ONION
1/2 TSP. WORCESTERSHIRE SAUCE
PINCH OF CAYENNE PEPPER

PUREE SOYBEANS—COMBINE WITH HALF AND HALF. ADD BOUILLON CUBES AND ONION TO BOILING WATER. THEN ADD SOYBEAN-CREAM MIXTURE, SLOWLY STIRRING UNTIL HOT. ADD PINCH OF CAYENNE. SERVE HOT.

BACON BITS OR CRUMBLED FRIED BACON MAKES A TASTY ADDITION TO THIS SOUP. ADD JUST BEFORE SERVING.

SERVES: 4-6
PROTEIN: 79 GRAMS

NORWEGIAN SOUP

2 C. DRIED SOYBEANS
2 QUARTS WATER
1 TSP. SALT
1 MEATY BEEF BONE
1 1/2 C. CHOPPED CELERY
1 1/2 C. CHOPPED ONIONS
3 TURNIPS DICED
1/4 C. CHOPPED PARSLEY
1/8 TSP. CAYENNE PEPPER
1/2 C. VINEGAR
1 LARGE CAN (28 OZ.) WHOLE TOMATOES
OR
4 LARGE FRESH TOMATOES

PUT ALL INGREDIENTS IN PRESSURE COOKER. COOK UNDER PRESSURE FOR 1 HOUR. IF YOU DO NOT HAVE A PRESSURE COOKER, USE METHOD NO. 2 (PAGE 1). SO FILLING AND HEARTY.

SERVES: 6
PROTEIN: 177 GRAMS

SIMPLE SOYBEANS

2 C. COOKED SOYBEANS
6 TBS. MARGARINE OR BUTTER
1/4 TSP. COARSE GROUND PEPPER

HEAT SOYBEANS, WITHOUT LID UNTIL ALMOST ALL LIQUID HAS EVAPORATED. WHILE STILL HOT ADD MARGARINE OR BUTTER. SPRINKLE WITH COARSE GROUND PEPPER. SERVE AS A SIDE DISH.

SERVES: 4
PROTEIN: 66 GRAMS

HOLIDAY STUFFING

4 C. COOKED SOYBEANS — MASHED
1 C. CHOPPED CELERY
1 C. CHOPPED ONION
1 C. MINCED WALNUTS
1/2 C. SESEME SEED
1 TSP. DILL SEED
1 TSP. OREGANO
1/2 TSP. POWDERED SAGE
2 EGGS BEATEN
PINCH OF SALT

COMBINE ALL INGREDIENTS. MIX WELL. STUFF YOUR TURKEY CHICKEN OR BEEF HEART.

IF YOU WISH TO SERVE THIS AS A SIDE DISH........
........ADD 1/2 C. POULTRY BROTH...
...OR 1/2 C. MELTED BUTTER

BAKE AT 350° FOR 30 MINUTES.

SERVES: 6
PROTEIN: 179 GRAMS

PILAF

1 CUBE MARGARINE
2 CUBES CHICKEN BOUILLON
2 C. WATER
1 C. SOYBEANS—COOKED
1 C. BROWN RICE

IN A HEAVY SKILLET- MELT MARGARINE, ADD BOUILLON CUBES AND WATER. STIR UNTIL BOUILLON HAS DISSOLVED. ADD RICE AND SOYBEANS. COVER SKILLET AND SIMMER FOR 45 MINUTES.

SERVES: 4-6
PROTEIN: 40 GRAMS

SOYBEANS'N SOUR CREAM

3 C. COOKED SOYBEANS
1/2 C. CHOPPED CHIVES
1/4 C. BACON BITS
1 C. SOUR CREAM

HEAT BEANS UNTIL HEATED THROUGH. DRAIN OFF ALL LIQUID. ADD ALL OTHER INGREDIENTS AND STIR AGAIN UNTIL HEATED THROUGH.

SERVES: 4
PROTEIN: 113 GRAMS

ITALIAN BEANS

2 C. COOKED SOYBEANS—WITH BROTH
2 C. GREEN BEANS
1 TSP. ROSEMARY
1/2 C. OLIVE OIL
1 CAN (8 OZ) TOMATO SAUCE
1 CLOVE GARLIC—MINCED

SIMMER ALL INGREDIENTS TOGETHER UNTIL THE BROTH HAS BECOME VERY THICK AND MOST OF THE LIQUID HAS EVAPORATED. STIR OFTEN.

SERVES: 4-6
PROTEIN: 80 GRAMS

MEXICAN BEANS

2 C. COOKED SOYBEANS—DRAINED
4 OZ. CHOPPED GREEN CHILES
1 C. CHILI SALSA
2 TSP. CHILI POWDER
1/4 TSP. CUMIN
1 C. GRATED JACK CHEESE

PUT IN SAUCE PAN ON MEDIUM LOW HEAT. STIR OFTEN—COOKING UNTIL MOST OF THE LIQUID HAS EVAPORATED. SERVE HOT AND BUBBLY.

SERVES: 4-6
PROTEIN: 94 GRAMS

FRIJOLES

3 C. COOKED SOYBEANS — DRAINED
1 C. MINCED ONIONS
1/2 C. MINCED GREEN PEPPER
1 C. GRATED CHEESE

MASH SOYBEANS. HEAT OIL IN A SKILLET AND SAUTE ONIONS AND GREEN PEPPER. ADD SOYBEANS, STIRRING UNTIL HOT. JUST BEFORE SERVING STIR IN THE GRATED CHEESE.

SERVES: 4-6
PROTEIN: 123 GRAMS

SOYBEANS AU GRATIN

3 C. SOYBEANS - COOKED
2 TBS. PARSLEY CHOPPED
1 TSP. BASIL
2. C. GRATED CHEDDAR CHEESE
1/4 C. POWDERED MILK

HEAT BEANS — THEN DRAIN OFF EXCESS LIQUID. ADD OTHER INGREDIENTS AND HEAT ON MEDIUM-LOW UNTIL BUBBLY.

SERVES: 4-6
PROTEIN: 154 GRAMS

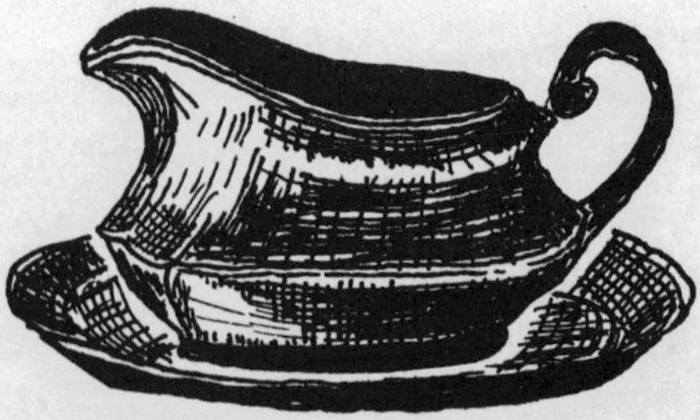

CREOLE

2 C. DRIED SOYBEANS
5 C. WATER
1 CAN (28 OZ.) WHOLE TOMATOES
..OR..
4 FRESH TOMATOES
2 C. CORN
1 C. MINCED BELL PEPPER
1 C. CHOPPED ONION
1/4 C. OLIVE OIL
1 TSP. VINEGAR
DASH CAYENNE PEPPER
2 TSP. SALT

TOSS EVERYTHING INTO A PRESSURE COOKER AND LET STEAM AWAY FOR AN HOUR. IF YOU DO NOT HAVE A PRESSURE COOKER, FOLLOW METHOD NUMBER 2 ON PAGE 1. LET SIT OVERNIGHT IN THE REFRIGERATOR TO BLEND FLAVORS.

SERVES: 6-8
PROTEIN: 173 GRAMS

SOYBEAN OMELET

1/2 C. COOKED SOYBEANS DRAINED
2 EGGS
1/4 TSP. SALT
1/4 TSP. CINNAMON
1/8 TSP. PEPPER
2 TBS. MINCED ONIONS
2 TBS. MINCED BELL PEPPER
1 C. GRATED JACK CHEESE

PUREE SOYBEANS. BEAT TOGETHER WITH EGGS, SALT, PEPPER, AND CINNAMON. POUR INTO A HOT GREASED 9 INCH SKILLET. LOWER HEAT TO MEDIUM — PUT LID ON AND STEAM FOR 3 OR 4 MINUTES, UNTIL TOP IS ALMOST FIRM. SPREAD ONIONS, BELL PEPPER, AND CHEESE OVER ONE COMPLETE HALF OF EGGS IN SKILLET. GENTLY FOLD OTHER HALF OVER. COVER AGAIN AND STEAM UNTIL CHEESE IS MELTED. TURN ONTO A PLATTER AND CUT INTO THREE OR FOUR PIECES. THIS IS BEAUTIFUL TOPPED WITH SOUR CREAM OR CHILI SALSA. EXPERIMENT WITH THE OMELET — ADD YOUR FAVORITE INGREDIENTS FOR ITS FILLING. WE SOMETIMES USE SOYBEAN FRIJOLES (PG. 28) OR CHORIZO (PG. 32) OR ZUCCHINI.

SERVES: 3-4
PROTEIN: 64 GRAMS

SKILLET SUPPER

2 C. COOKED SOYBEANS
1 1/2 C. CORN
1 CAN (28 OZ.) WHOLE TOMATOES
3/4 C. CHOPPED ONIONS
1/2 TSP. CELERY SEED
1/2 TSP. COARSE GROUND PEPPER
1/2 TSP. THYME
1/2 TSP. SALT
1/2 C. CORNMEAL
1 1/2 C. GRATED CHEDDAR CHEESE
DASH CAYENNE PEPPER

COMBINE ALL INGREDIENTS AND PUT IN A HEAVY SKILLET. BAKE AT 350° FOR 45 MINUTES.

SERVES: 6
PROTEIN: 76 GRAMS

SOY WELSH RAREBIT

1 1/2 C. COOKED SOYBEANS – DRAINED
2 TBS. OIL
2 TBS. WHOLE WHEAT FLOUR
1/2 TSP. SALT
2 C. MILK
1 1/2 C. CHEDDAR CHEESE – GRATED
1 EGG, WELL BEATEN
1/4 C. WHITE WINE

HEAT OIL. BLEND IN FLOUR AND SALT. SLOWLY ADD MILK, WHILE STIRRING, THEN ADD GRATED CHEESE. STIR UNTIL THICK. POUR A LITTLE SAUCE INTO THE BEATEN EGG, MIX, THEN POUR ALL BACK INTO THE SAUCE. ADD SOYBEANS AND SIMMER UNTIL HEATED THROUGH. SERVE OVER TOAST.

SERVES: 4
PROTEIN: 119 GRAMS

DELIA'S SWEET'N SOUR

5 C. COOKED SOYBEANS
2 LARGE ONIONS CUT IN 1" PIECES
3 LARGE CARROTS CUT IN 1/8" SLICES
1 CLOVE GARLIC MINCED
2 GREEN PEPPERS – THINLY SLICED

<u>SAUCE</u>...... STIR TOGETHER UNTIL BUBBLING....
1/4 C. CORNSTARCH
1 C. BROWN SUGAR OR 2/3 C. HONEY
1 TSP. GINGER
1/2 TSP. CINNAMON
1/4 C. SOY SAUCE
1/2 C. VINEGAR
1/2 C. SOYBEAN STOCK
2 C. PINEAPPLE CHUNKS WITH JUICE

WHEN SAUCE IS BUBBLING, ADD SOYBEANS AND HEAT THROUGH, STIRRING OFTEN. ADD VEGETABLES – BUT TAKE PAN OFF BURNER. LET SIT IN THE REFRIGERATOR FOR SEVERAL HOURS OR OVERNIGHT FOR A PROPER BLENDING OF FLAVORS REHEAT JUST BEFORE SERVING. DO NOT OVERCOOK VEGETABLES SHOULD BE CRISP.

SERVES: 6-8
PROTEIN: 170 GRAMS

MUSAKA

2 1/2 C. COOKED SOYBEANS
2 MEDIUM EGGPLANTS
3/4 C. CHOPPED ONION
1/2 TSP. THYME
1/2 TSP. OREGANO
1 TSP. SALT
1 TSP. MINCED GARLIC
1 CAN (6 OZ.) TOMATO PASTE
3 EGGS BEATEN
3 C. GRATED CHEDDAR CHEESE

PREPARE THIS RECIPE A DAY AHEAD......... CUT EGGPLANTS IN FOURTHS. PLACE IN A BAKING DISH—BRUSH WITH OIL. BAKE AT 400° FOR 24 MINUTES UNTIL MEAT OF EGGPLANT IS TENDER. PEEL OFF SKINS AND CUT EGGPLANT INTO CUBES. SAUTE ONIONS. ADD SPICES, TOMATO PASTE, SOYBEANS, AND CUBED EGGPLANT. WHEN MIXTURE IS HOT-ADD EGGS. PUT 1/3 OF MIXTURE IN A GREASED 2 1/2 QUART CASSEROLE. TOP WITH 1 CUP OF CHEESE. REPEAT TWO MORE TIMES. YOUR MUSAKA IS READY FOR TOMORROW ....BEFORE SERVING POP INTO THE OVEN AT 350° FOR 45 MINUTES.

SERVES: 6-8
PROTEIN: 192 GRAMS

VEGETABLE PATTIES

1 1/4 C. MASHED SOYBEANS
2 EGGS BEATEN
1/3 C. CHOPPED GREEN PEPPER
1/3 C. DICED CELERY
1 1/2 C. THINLY SLICED ZUCCHINI
1/3 C. CHOPPED ONION
1 C. GRATED CARROT
1/4 TSP. CINNAMON
1/4 TSP. DILL
1/4 TSP. SALT
DASH OF CAYENNE PEPPER

COMBINE ALL INGREDIENTS. MAKE INTO PATTIES—THEY WILL BE MUSHY. FRY AT MEDIUM HEAT IN A GREASED SKILLET. SERVE WITH CHILI SALSA OR SOUR CREAM.....OR.... MAKE AN OPEN FACE SANDWICH—PUTTING PATTY ON A TOASTED WHOLE WHEAT BUN—TOP WITH SPROUTS AND SOUR CREAM.

MAKES: 6-8 PATTIES
PROTEIN: 72 GRAMS

BEAN SCALLOP

- 1/4 C. OIL
- 1/2 C. GREEN PEPPERS — MINCED
- 1/2 C. ONION — MINCED
- 2 TBS. PARSLEY
- 1/4 TSP. CUMIN
- 1/2 TSP. SALT
- 1/4 TSP. COARSE PEPPER
- 1/3 C. WHOLE WHEAT FLOUR
- 1 2/3 C. EVAPORATED MILK
- 1/2 C. LIQUID DRAINED FROM BEANS
- 2 C. SOYBEANS
- 1 1/2 C. GRATED JACK CHEESE
- 1/2 C. WHOLE WHEAT BREAD CRUMBS

BROWN ONIONS AND GREEN PEPPER IN OIL. BLEND IN FLOUR AND SPICES. GRADUALLY ADD LIQUIDS, STIRRING CONSTANTLY, UNTIL THICK AS GRAVY. TAKE OFF BURNER AND STIR IN CHEESE. COMBINE SOYBEANS AND SAUCE. PUT IN A 9 x 9 GREASED BAKING PAN. TOP WITH BREAD CRUMBS JUST BEFORE BAKING. BAKE AT 350° FOR 30 MINUTES.

SERVES: 6-8
PROTEIN: 148 GRAMS

HUNGARIANS

1 C. COOKED SOYBEANS
1 C. COOKED BROWN RICE
1 EGG BEATEN
1/2 TSP. DILL SEED
1/2 TSP. ALLSPICE
1/4 TSP. SALT
1/4 TSP COARSE GROUND PEPPER
2 TBS. GREEN ONIONS CHOPPED
1 CAN, 8 OZ., TOMATO SAUCE
2 TBS OLIVE OIL
8-10 CABBAGE LEAVES

MASH SOYBEANS—COMBINE WITH RICE, EGG, SPICES, AND ONION. PUT CABBAGE LEAVES IN BOILING WATER FOR TWO OR THREE MINUTES, UNTIL LEAVES ARE LIMP. ROLL SOYBEAN MIXTURE INTO A BALL AND WRAP IN A CABBAGE LEAF. PLACE EACH ROLL CLOSE TOGETHER IN A LOAF PAN. COMBINE TOMATO SAUCE AND OLIVE OIL AND POUR OVER CABBAGE ROLLS. BAKE AT 350° FOR 30 MINUTES.

SERVES: 4-6
PROTEIN: 60 GRAMS

SOYBEAN CURRY

- 3 C. COOKED SOYBEANS
- 1 C. CELERY—DICED
- 1 ONION—FINELY CHOPPED
- 1/2 C. CARROT—DICED
- 3/4 C. BELL PEPPER—MINCED
- 1 C. CRUSHED PINEAPPLE—WITH JUICE
- 1/2 C. RAISINS
- 1/2 C. SHREDDED COCOANUT
- 1/2 C. BROWN SUGAR OR HONEY
- 1 TBS. FLOUR
- 1 TBS. CURRY POWDER
- 1/4 TSP. GINGER
- 1/4 TSP. SALT

SAUTE GARLIC, CELERY, ONION, CARROT, AND BELLPEPPER. ADD SOYBEANS AND ALL OTHER INGREDIENTS. HEAT—STIRRING UNTIL HOT. REFRIGERATE OVERNIGHT FOR FLAVORS TO BLEND. REHEAT AND SERVE.

SERVES: 4-6
PROTEIN: 104 GRAMS

SOYBEANS OLÉ

- 1 1/2 C. COOKED SOYBEANS—MASHED
- 1/2 C. CHOPPED GREEN CHILES
- 1 C. GRATED JACK CHEESE
- 1/2 C. MINCED ONION
- 1/2 TSP. CUMIN
- 1/8 TSP. SALT
- 3/4 TSP. CHILI POWDER
- 3 EGGS-BEATEN

BEAT EGGS AND SOYBEANS TOGETHER, LEAVING SOYBEANS IN SMALL LUMPS. ADD TO OTHER INGREDIENTS AND POUR INTO A 2 1/2 QUART GREASED CASSEROLE. BAKE AT 350° FOR 35 MINUTES. SERVE WITH CHILI SALSA OR HOT SAUCE.

SERVES: 4-6
PROTEIN: 106 GRAMS

ENCHILADA PIE

2 1/2 C. COOKED SOYBEANS
1 1/2 TSP. CHILI POWDER
3/4 TSP. CUMIN
1/2 TSP. SALT
2 TBS. OIL
1 CAN (15 OZ.) TOMATO SAUCE
1/2 C. CHOPPED ONION
1/2 C. DICED GREEN CHILES (4 OZ. CAN)
1/2 C. SLICED OLIVES (4 OZ. CAN)
1/2 POUND CHEDDAR CHEESE – GRATED
6 TO 8 CORN TORTILLAS

BROWN ONIONS IN OIL. ADD SPICES, SOYBEANS, TOMATO SAUCE, CHILES, AND OLIVES. STIR TIL HOT. LET SIT FOR SEVERAL HOURS, OR OVERNIGHT IN REFRIGERATOR, FOR FLAVORS TO BLEND. JUST BEFORE BAKING – GREASE A 2 1/2 QUART CASSEROLE. PUT IN A LAYER OF TORTILLAS, 1/3 OF BEAN MIXTURE, THEN 1/3 OF GRATED CHEESE. REPEAT TWO MORE TIMES. BAKE AT 350° FOR 35 MINUTES.

SERVES: 6-8
PROTEIN: 136 GRAMS

MUSHROOM LOAF

2 C. COOKED SOYBEANS
1 C. SLICED MUSHROOMS
1/2 C. CHOPPED CELERY
1/2 C. MILK
1 EGG BEATEN
1 C. WHOLE WHEAT BREAD CRUMBS
1/2 TSP. SALT
1/8 TSP. SAVORY

COMBINE ALL INGREDIENTS AND PLACE IN LOAF PAN. BAKE AT 350° FOR 30 MINUTES OR UNTIL LOAF IS FIRM. TURN OUT ON PLATTER AND SERVE.

SERVES: 6
PROTEIN: 97 GRAMS

FRIJOLES SUPREMÉ

12 TORTILLAS
3 C. FRIJOLES — PAGE 17
1 TSP. CHILI POWDER
1/4 TSP. CUMIN
1/4 C. CHOPPED GREEN CHILES

BRUSH TORTILLAS WITH OIL AND BAKE AT 350° FOR 5 MINUTES UNTIL CRISP. COMBINE FRIJOLES WITH CHILI POWDER, CUMIN AND GREEN CHILES. SPREAD MIXTURE ON EACH TORTILLA AND POP UNDER THE BROILER. SERVE HOT WITH ANY OR ALL OF THE TOPPINGS AS SIDE DISHES.

SERVES: 6-8
PROTEIN: 130 GRAMS

TOPPINGS

CHOPPED TOMATOES
SPROUTS
SHREDDED LETTUCE
SOUR CREAM
MASHED AVOCADO

A FEAST (WHEN FARMER COURTER, FROM DOWN THE ROAD, GAVE US SOME OF HIS HOMEGROWN SPARERIBS WE COULDN T RESIST TRYING THEM WITH SOYBEANS ___)

5 C. COOKED SOYBEANS WITH LIQUID
12 PORK SPARERIBS
1 CAN (20 OZ.) CRUSHED PINEAPPLE
1 CAN (15 OZ.) TOMATO SAUCE
1 1/4 C. DARK BROWN SUGAR PACKED

COMBINE TOMATO SAUCE, PINEAPPLE, AND BROWN SUGAR. PUT SPARERIBS IN A LARGE BAKING DISH AND COVER WITH THE SAUCE. BAKE AT 325° FOR 1 1/4 HOURS TURNING THE SPARERIBS AT LEAST ONCE. THEN ADD THE SOYBEANS SPOONING THE SAUCE OVER THEM UNTIL THEY ARE COATED. BAKE FOR ANOTHER 1 1/4 HOURS STIRRING AND BASTING OCCASIONALLY. THE SAUCE WILL BE DARK AND THICK AND THE SPARERIBS SO TENDER.

SERVES: 6
PROTEIN: 205 GRAMS

BAKED BEANS

RICH AND DELICIOUS

5 C. COOKED SOYBEANS, WITH BROTH
1 LARGE ONION — MINCED
2 TSP. DRY MUSTARD
3/4 C. MOLASSES
1/4 C. HONEY
5 SLICES BACON — CHOPPED

COMBINE ALL INGREDIENTS. BAKE IN AN UNCOVERED 2 1/2 QUART CASSEROLE AT 325° FOR 2 1/2 HOURS. STIR OCCASIONALLY ADD A LITTLE WATER, IF NECESSARY, DURING BAKING.

SERVES: 6-8
PROTEIN: 171 GRAMS

FOR AN EXQUISITE VARIATION, ADD TWO CUPS OF CORN DURING THE LAST 30 MINUTES OF BAKING. JUST BEFORE SERVING TOP WITH 2 CUPS OF GRATED JACK CHEESE. POP BACK INTO THE OVEN UNTIL THE CHEESE MELTS — THEN SERVE.

PROTEIN: 219 GRAMS

HAM'n BEANS

PERFECT ON A COLD DAY

USE BASIC SOYBEAN RECIPE — THROW A A HAM BONE AND 1 DICED ONION IN WITH THE BEANS. SERVE WITH HEARTY CORN MUFFINS (RECIPE ON PAGE 44).

SERVES: 6-8
PROTEIN: 165 GRAMS

IF YOU LIKE LASAGNE — YOU'LL BE WILD ABOUT THIS RECIPE —

MOCK LASAGNE

5 C. COOKED SOYBEAN
1/2 POUND GROUND BEEF
1/2 TSP. OREGANO
14 OZ. TOMATO SAUCE
1 C. SOUR CREAM
1 C. COTTAGE CHEESE
8 OZ. CREAM CHEESE
1/2 C. GREEN ONION CHOPPED
2 TBS. BELL PEPPER CHOPPED

BROWN HAMBURGER AND COMBINE WITH BEANS, OREGANO, AND TOMATO SAUCE.
IN A BOWL BEAT SOUR CREAM, COTTAGE CHEESE, AND CREAM CHEESE TOGETHER. ADD GREEN ONIONS AND BELL PEPPER TO THE CHEESES. LAYER IN A 2 QUART CASSEROLE 1/4 OF THE BEANS THEN 1/3 OF THE CHEESE MIXTURE. KEEP REPEATING, ENDING WITH THE BEAN MIXTURE ON TOP. POP INTO THE OVEN AT 350° FOR 30 MINUTES OR UNTIL BUBBLY.

SERVES: 6-8
PROTEIN: 271 GRAMS

CHORIZO

3 C. COOKED SOYBEANS
12 OZ. BEEF CHORIZO
1/2 C. ONION - MINCED
1/2 C. TOMATO SAUCE
1 CLOVE GARLIC - CRUSHED

BROWN ONION GARLIC AND CHORIZO. ADD BEANS AND TOMATO SAUCE AND HEAT THROUGH. REFRIGERATE FOR SEVERAL HOURS OR OVER-NIGHT. REHEAT AND SERVE.

SERVES: 4-6
PROTEIN: 113 GRAMS

EVERYONE ASKS FOR THIS RECIPE WHEN WE SERVE IT. WE SERVE HOT BOWLS OF CHORIZO WITH HOT BUTTERED TORTILLAS AND A BIG GREEN SALAD. SO GOOD!

WIENERS 'N BEANS YUMM!

3 C. COOKED SOYBEANS
1/2 C. MOLASSES
1 1/2 TBS. DRY MUSTARD
1 TBS. WORCESTERSHIRE
6 FRANKFURTERS — MORE IF YOU LIKE
DASH CAYENNE

SLICE FRANKFURTERS 1/2 INCH THICK. COMBINE ALL INGREDIENTS IN A 2 QUART CASSEROLE. BAKE AT 325° FOR 2 1/2 HOURS. STIR OCCASIONALLY CHECKING TO SEE IF YOU NEED TO ADD LIQUID.

SERVES: 4-6
PROTEIN: 141 GRAMS

CHUCK WAGON BEANS

2 C. DRIED SOYBEANS
5 C. WATER
2 ONIONS - CHOPPED
1 GREEN PEPPER - CHOPPED
3 CLOVES GARLIC - MINCED
3 TBS. CHILI POWDER
1 TSP. GROUND CUMIN
1/2 POUND HAMBURGER
1 1/2 TSP. SALT
1 DRIED HOT PEPPER - CHOPPED (WITH SEEDS)
2 CANS (8 OZ.) TOMATO SAUCE

PUT ALL INGREDIENTS IN PRESSURE COOKER AND COOK FOR 1 1/4 HOURS. IF YOU DONT HAVE A PRESSURE COOKER USE METHOD 2, PAGE 1.

SERVES: 6-8
PROTEIN: 221 GRAMS

FLOUR REPLACEMENT

FOR IMPROVED FLAVOR AND NOURISHMENT IN RECIPES USE UP TO 1 PART SOY FLOUR TO 2 PARTS OTHER FLOUR WHEREVER FLOUR IS USED. AT WILDERNESS HOUSE WE GO ONE STEP FURTHER. WE REPLACE THAT SOY FLOUR WITH COOKED SOYBEANS.

THIS IS THE FORMULA:

1. 1/2 C. COOKED DRAINED SOYBEANS = 1/3 C. SOY FLOUR.
2. DECREASE THE LIQUID IN YOUR RECIPE BY 2 TABLESPOONS FOR EACH 1/2 C. COOKED SOYBEANS YOU USE.

WE ARE INCLUDING ONLY A FEW BREAD AND DESSERT RECIPES IN THIS BOOK TO SHOW THE VERSATILITY OF USING THE SOYBEAN AS A REPLACEMENT. EXPERIMENT — TRY IT IN YOUR FAVORITE RECIPES AND ADD MORE NUTRITION TO YOUR DIET FOR PENNIES.

POOR BOY'S CHEESECAKE

1/2 C. COOKED SOYBEANS — DRAINED
2 EGGS—BEATEN
8 OZ. CREAM CHEESE
1 C. SOUR CREAM
3/4 TSP. CINNAMON
1/4 TSP. SALT
5 TSP. LEMON JUICE
3 TBS. GRATED LEMON RIND
1/2 C. HONEY

PUREE SOYBEANS. BEAT WELL WITH OTHER INGREDIENTS. POUR INTO A GRAHAM CRACKER CRUST AND BAKE AT 350° FOR 45 MINUTES. CHILL BEFORE SERVING.

GRAHAM CRACKER CRUST

1 C. GRAHAM CRACKER CRUMBS
2/3 C. MARGARINE
1/2 TSP. CINNAMON
1 1/2 TBS. HONEY

COMBINE INGREDIENTS AND PRESS DOWN FIRMLY IN BOTTOM OF 8" CAKE PAN.

SERVES: 6-8
PROTEIN: 75 GRAMS

APPLESAUCE CAKE

1 1/2 C. COOKED SOYBEANS — DRAINED
1 C. BROWN SUGAR
1/2 C. OIL
4 EGGS — WELL BEATEN
3/4 C. APPLESAUCE
2 C. WHOLE WHEAT FLOUR
1/2 C. POWDERED MILK
4 TSP. BAKING POWDER
1 TSP. SALT
2 1/2 TSP. CINNAMON
1 1/2 C. RAISINS

PUREE SOYBEANS. BEAT TOGETHER WITH BROWN SUGAR, OIL, EGGS, AND APPLESAUCE. COMBINE DRY INGREDIENTS. BLEND ALL TOGETHER WITH RAISINS. TURN INTO A WELL GREASED 12 x 8 PAN — BAKE AT 350° FOR 40 MINUTES.

SERVES: 16
PROTEIN: 143 GRAMS

TO ENHANCE THIS LUCIOUS CAKE TRY OUR WILDERNESS HOUSE GLAZE.

WILDERNESS HOUSE GLAZE

1/3 C. HONEY
1 TBS. WATER
2 TBS. GRATED ORANGE PEEL

COMBINE INGREDIENTS. PUNCTURE HOT CAKE WITH A FORK AND DRIZZLE THE GLAZE OVER THE TOP.

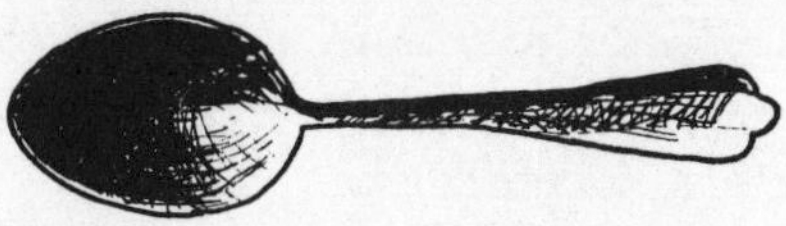

SPOON CAKE

1 1/2 C. COOKED SOYBEANS—DRAINED
1/2 C. RAW OR BROWN SUGAR
1 TBS. CONCENTRATED ORANGE JUICE
1/2 C. WHOLE CREAM
1/4 TSP. SALT
1/4 TSP. BAKING SODA
1 1/2 TSP. BAKING POWDER
1 1/2 TSP. CINNAMON
1 TSP VANILLA
2 EGGS BEATEN

PUREE SOYBEANS. BEAT TOGETHER ALL OTHER INGREDIENTS. SLOWLY BEAT INTO PUREED SOYBEANS. POUR INTO A 9" CAKE PAN, WELL GREASED. BAKE AT 350° FOR 30 MINUTES. WE LOVE THIS WARM! SOOO-GOOD SERVED PLAIN OR TOPPED WITH A VANILLA FROSTING. CUT INTO WEDGES OR SPOON INTO BOWLS.

SERVES: 6-8
PROTEIN: 65 GRAMS

PEANUT BUTTER COOKIES

1 C. COOKED SOYBEANS – DRAINED
1/2 C. MARGARINE
1/2 C. BROWN SUGAR, PACKED
1/2 C. HONEY
3/4 C. CHUNK STYLE PEANUT BUTTER
1 C. WHOLE WHEAT FLOUR
1/4 TSP. SALT
1 1/2 TSP. BAKING POWDER

PUREE SOYBEANS – CREAM TOGETHER WITH MARGARINE, HONEY, BROWN SUGAR, AND PEANUT BUTTER. COMBINE WITH DRY INGREDIENTS. CHILL. BATTER WILL BE A BIT STICKY SO CAREFULLY ROLL INTO BALLS. PLACE ON A GREASED COOKIE SHEET AND FLATTEN WITH A FORK DIPPED IN FLOUR. BAKE AT 350° FOR ABOUT 15 MINUTES.

3 DOZEN COOKIES
PROTEIN: 99 GRAMS

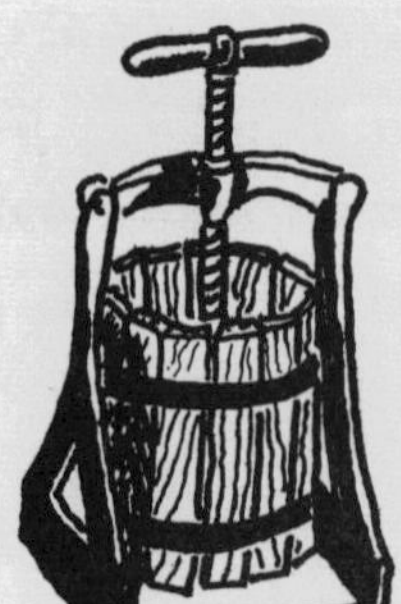

GOLDEN COOKIE NUGGETS

1 1/2 COOKED SOYBEANS — DRAINED
3/4 C. HONEY
3/4 C. MARGARINE
2 EGGS
2 1/2 C. OATMEAL
1 1/4 C. WHOLE WHEAT FLOUR
1/4 TSP. SALT
2 TSP. CINNAMON
1 1/4 TSP. BAKING POWDER
2 C. FINELY CHOPPED DATES

PUREE SOYBEANS. BEAT WITH MARGARINE, HONEY, EGGS. ADD COMBINED DRY INGREDIENTS — THEN THE DATES. DROP BY TEASPOONFULS ON A GREASED COOKIE SHEET. BAKE AT 350° FOR 20 MINUTES.

3 DOZEN COOKIES
PROTEIN: 99 GRAMS

CANDY BALLS

1/2 C. COOKED SOYBEANS — DRAINED
1/2 C. HONEY
1/2 C. SUNFLOWER SEEDS
1/2 C. SESAME SEEDS
1/2 C. CHOPPED DATES
1/2 C. COCOANUT
1 TSP. CINNAMON

ROLL INTO BALLS AND REFRIGERATE. (A BIT STICKY BUT SO GOOD AND HEALTHY YOU WON T EVEN CARE IF THE KIDS SNITCH THIS FOR BREAKFAST.) YOU MIGHT WANT TO ROLL THEM IN NUTS, SESAME SEEDS OR COCOANUT. OURS ALWAYS DISAPPEAR BEFORE WE HAVE A CHANCE TO ROLL THEM IN ANYTHING!

CANDYBALLS 12-16
PROTEIN: 42 GRAMS

PIE PASTRY

2/3 C. SOYBEANS — PUREED
1/4 C. SOFT MARGARINE OR BUTTER
1/2 C. WHOLE WHEAT FLOUR
1/2 TSP. CINNAMON
PINCH OF SALT

COMBINE ALL INGREDIENTS. ROLL INTO A BALL AND REFRIGERATE FOR 30 MINUTES. ROLL OUT ON FLOURED BOARD UNTIL VERY THIN. LINE PIE PAN PUNCTURING SIDES AND BOTTOM WITH A FORK. BAKE AT 450° FOR 10 MINUTES.

MAKES:	9 INCH SINGLE CRUST
PROTEIN:	28 GRAMS

SUZI'S PROTEIN BREAD

1 1/2 C. COOKED SOYBEANS — DRAINED
2 CAKES FRESH YEAST
— OR —
2 PACKAGES DRY YEAST
1 C. LUKEWARM WATER
2 TBS. HONEY
1 1/2 TBS. OIL
3 C. WHOLE WHEAT FLOUR
1 1/2 TSP. SALT

PUREE SOYBEANS. DISSOLVE YEAST IN WARM WATER WITH HONEY. BEAT SOYBEANS INTO YEAST MIXTURE AND LET STAND FOR 20 MINUTES IN A VERY WARM PLACE, AROUND 80°. THEN ADD THE DRY INGREDIENTS THAT YOU HAVE COMBINED. KNEAD DOUGH UNTIL IT IS VERY ELASTIC. WHEN YOU PRESS IT WITH YOUR FINGER THE INDENTATION SHOULD POP BACK. MAKE A ROUND BALL OF THE DOUGH AND PUT IN AN OILED BOWL. TURN THE BALL SO THAT ALL SIDES GET LIGHTLY OILED. LET RISE IN A WARM PLACE UNTIL DOUBLED IN BULK. PUNCH DOWN SHAPE AND PUT IN A LARGE OILED LOAF PAN. LET RISE UNTIL DOUBLE IN BULK. PLACE IN A PREHEATED OVEN AT 350° AND BAKE FOR 1 1/4 HOURS.

BE CREATIVE — ADD 1/2 C. SPROUTED WHEAT OR 1/2 C. CRACKED WHEAT OR ANY OF YOUR FAVORITES TO THIS BREAD.

MAKES 1 LARGE LOAF
PROTEIN: 88 GRAMS

HOLIDAY LOAF

RIGHT FOR ANY HOLIDAY

1 C. COOKED SOYBEANS
1 C. HONEY
1/2 C. OIL
2 EGGS
1 TSP. CINNAMON
1 TSP. ALLSPICE
1 TSP. NUTMEG
1/2 TSP. SALT
1 1/2 C. WHOLE WHEAT FLOUR
1 TSP. BAKING POWDER
1/2 C. NUTS
1/2 C. CHOPPED DATES
1/2 C. RAISINS

PUREE SOYBEANS. BEAT WELL WITH HONEY, OIL, AND EGGS. COMBINE DRY INGREDIENTS. MIX WITH SOYBEAN MIXTURE. STIR IN NUTS, DATES, AND RAISINS. POUR INTO A LARGE LOAF PAN AND BAKE AT 350° FOR 1 HOUR AND 10 MINUTES.

MAKES: 1 LARGE LOAF
PROTEIN: 92 GRAMS

WE MAKE SEVERAL HOLIDAY LOAVES AT ONE TIME AND FREEZE THEM. THEN WE'RE READY FOR COMPANY.

PANCAKES

1 C. COOKED SOYBEANS — DRAINED
2 C. MILK
2 TBS. HONEY
1/4 C. OIL
2 EGGS - BEATEN
2 C. WHOLE WHEAT FLOUR
1 TBS. BAKING POWDER
1 TSP. BAKING SODA
3/4 TSP. SALT
1/2 TSP. CINNAMON
1/4 TSP. NUTMEG

PUREE SOYBEANS AND BEAT IN MILK, HONEY, OIL AND EGGS. COMBINE DRY INGREDIENTS. STIR SOYBEAN MIXTURE INTO DRY INGREDIENTS, BLENDING WELL BUT NOT BEATING TOO MUCH. POUR BATTER ON HOT GRIDDLE (400°) AND SPREAD OUT WITH A SPOON. BATTER WILL BE THICK BUT DON'T ADD MORE LIQUID. SOYBEAN PANCAKES TAKE LONGER TO COOK THAN ORDINARY PANCAKES — ABOUT 3 MINUTES ON EACH SIDE — BUT THEY COME OUT GOLDEN, FLUFFY, AND NUTRITIOUS.

SERVES: 6
PROTEIN: 99 GRAMS

HEARTY CORN MUFFINS

1 1/2 C. COOKED SOYBEANS
1/4 C. OIL
2 TBS. BROWN SUGAR
1 C. WATER
2 EGGS- WELL BEATEN
1 TSP. SALT
1 1/2 TSP CINNAMON
1 1/2 TSP. BAKING POWDER
1 1/2 C. CORN MEAL

PUREE SOYBEANS. BEAT IN OIL, BROWN SUGAR EGGS, AND WATER. COMBINE SPICES AND BAKING POWDER WITH CORN MEAL. PUT ALL INGREDIENTS TOGETHER. POUR INTO MUFFIN TIN LINED WITH MUFFIN PAPERS OR GREASE PAN GENEROUSLY. BAKE AT 400° FOR 40 MINUTES.

18 MUFFINS
PROTEIN: 85 GRAMS

VARIETY MUFFIN

2/3 C. COOKED SOYBEANS
2 EGGS
6 TBS. HONEY
1 1/2 C. BUTTERMILK
1 1/2 C. WHOLE WHEAT FLOUR
2 TSP. BAKING POWDER
1 TSP. SALT
1 TSP. CINNAMON
1/2 TSP. BAKING SODA

PUREE SOYBEANS. BEAT WITH HONEY, EGGS, AND BUTTERMILK. BLEND DRY INGREDIENTS IN ANOTHER BOWL. COMBINE ALL INGREDIENTS. ADD ANY, OR A COMBINATION, OF THE FOLLOWING

2/3 C. RAISINS
2/3 C. CHOPPED NUTS
2/3 C. COCOANUT
2 TBS. LEMON RIND GRATED

FILL WELL GREASED MUFFIN TINS 3/4 FULL. BAKE AT 350° FOR 45 MINUTES.

16-18 MUFFINS
PROTEIN: 84 GRAMS

SWEET MUFFINS

1 1/2 C. COOKED SOYBEANS— DRAINED
1 C. BROWN SUGAR
1/4 C. MARGARINE
2 EGGS SEPARATED
1/2 TSP. SALT
2 TSP. CINNAMON
2 TSP. BAKING POWDER
1/2 TSP. NUTMEG
1 1/2 C. WHOLE WHEAT FLOUR
1 C. RAISINS
1/2 C. GROUND TOASTED SOYBEANS—
— OPTIONAL

PUREE SOYBEANS AND BEAT TOGETHER WITH 3/4 CUP BROWN SUGAR, MARGARINE AND EGG YOLKS. BEAT EGG WHITES UNTIL STIFF, SLOWLY ADDING THE OTHER 1/4 CUP BROWN SUGAR. ADD SPICES TO FLOUR AND BLEND. COMBINE FLOUR MIXTURE WITH SOYBEAN MIXTURE THEN FOLD IN EGG WHITES THEN RAISINS AND GROUND SOYBEANS. FILL WELL GREASED MUFFIN TIN 3/4 FULL. BAKE AT 350° FOR 45 MINUTES.

12-16 MUFFINS
PROTEIN: 85 GRAMS

SOYBEAN CREPE FOR THE ADVENTUROUS

4 EGGS
2/3 C. DRAINED SOYBEANS (COOKED)
2 TBS. HONEY

........FOR DESSERT CREPE.......
ADD 2 TSP. CINNAMON

........FOR MAIN DISH CREPE.........
ADD 1/2 TSP. CELERY SEED
1/4 TSP. DILL SEED

PUREE ALL INGREDIENTS IN A BLENDER. USE THE BACKSIDE OF A SMOOTH BOTTOMED SKILLET AS YOUR COOKING SURFACE. HEAT THE SKILLET—UPSIDE DOWN—OVER MEDIUM HEAT. OIL THE BACKSIDE LIGHTLY. PLACE ABOUT 2 TABLESPOONS OF BATTER ON THE BACK OF THE SKILLET AND QUICKLY SPREAD WITH A SPOON UNTIL THIN AND ROUND. HEAT FOR 45 TO 60 SECONDS UNTIL THE EDGES OF YOUR CREPE ARE BROWN. SLIGHTLY LOOSEN THE ENTIRE EDGE OF YOUR CREPE WITH A SPATULA, THEN GENTLY PEEL THE CREPE OFF. TURN IT OVER AND COOK FOR AN ADDITIONAL 20 SECONDS. WIPE SKILLET LIGHTLY WITH OIL BETWEEN MAKING EACH CREPE. STACK CREPES BETWEEN SHEETS OF WAXED PAPER.

MAKES: 10-12 CREPES

CREPE FILLINGS

......DESSERT CREPE FILLINGS..........

BERRIES
APPLESAUCE
YOGURT
PINEAPPLE
PUDDINGS

SPREAD FILLING ONTO THE CREPE THEN GENTLY ROLL IT UP. GARNISH WITH SOUR CREAM OR DRIZZLE HONEY OVER THE TOP.

......MAIN DISH CREPE FILLINGS.............

SOYBEANS AU GRATIN - PAGE 18.
MEAT IN A WHITE SAUCE
VEGETABLES IN A WHITE SAUCE
SEAFOODS IN A WHITE SAUCE
TUNA SALAD
CHICKEN SALAD
PICNIC SALAD - PAGE 8.

——— BE CREATIVE ———

SPOON FILLING ONTO THE CREPE AND GENTLY FOLD TOGETHER. GARNISH WITH A CHEESE SAUCE OR A HOLLANDAISE SAUCE. FOR HOT CREPE DISHES SLIP THE FINISHED CREPE UNDER THE BROILER FOR A MINUTE OR TWO.

SOYBEANS ARE ONE OF THE MOST INEXPENSIVE, NUTRITIONAL FOODS KNOWN TO MAN. THE PROBLEM IS LARGELY A MATTER OF TASTE. YET, THIS BEAN THAT CAN FEED THE WORLD CAN BE DELIGHTFULLY APPETIZING! ....THIS IS WHAT SOYBEAN COOKERY IS ALL ABOUT.